12 QUESTIONS ABOUT THE
DECLARATION
OF INDEPENDENCE

by Mirella S. Miller

12 STORY LIBRARY

www.12StoryLibrary.com

12-Story Library is an imprint of Peterson Publishing Company and Press Room Editions.

Produced for 12-Story Library by Red Line Editorial

Photographs ©: Todd Taulman/Shutterstock Images, cover, 1; duncan1890/iStockphoto, 4; Library of Congress, 5, 9, 22; North Wind Picture Archives, 6; North Wind Picture Archives/AP Images, 7, 29; HultonArchive/iStockphoto, 8, 14, 18; oversnap/iStockphoto, 10; David Smart/Shutterstock Images, 11; AP Images, 12, 25, 28; GeorgiosArt/iStockphoto, 13; juliaf/iStockphoto, 15; Everett Historical/Shutterstock Images, 16, 19, 21; ziggymaj/iStockphoto, 17; pictore/iStockphoto, 20; Joseph Sohm/Shutterstock Images, 24; franckreporter/iStockphoto, 26; kreicher/iStockphoto, 27

Library of Congress Cataloging-in-Publication Data
Names: Miller, Mirella S., author.
Title: 12 questions about the Declaration of Independence / by Mirella S.
  Miller.
Other titles: Twelve questions about the Declaration of Independence
Description: Mankato, MN : 12-Story Library, 2017 | Series: Examining
  primary sources | Includes bibliographical references and index. |
  Audience: Grades 4-6.
Identifiers: LCCN 2016002326 (print) | LCCN 2016002593 (ebook) | ISBN
  9781632352835 (library bound : alk. paper) | ISBN 9781632353337 (pbk. :
  alk. paper) | ISBN 9781621434504 (hosted ebook)
Subjects: LCSH: United States. Declaration of Independence--Juvenile
  literature. | United States--Politics and government--1775-1783--Juvenile
  literature.
Classification: LCC E221 .M64 2016 (print) | LCC E221 (ebook) | DDC
  973.3/13--dc23
LC record available at http://lccn.loc.gov/2016002326

Printed in the United States of America
Mankato, MN
January, 2018

Access free, up-to-date content on this topic plus a full digital version of this book. Scan the QR code on page 31 or use your school's login at 12StoryLibrary.com.

Table of Contents

1

What Was Happening in 1775?

In the eighteenth century, the 13 colonies in America were under British rule. The British traded goods with the colonists. King George III of England and the British Parliament required colonists to pay small taxes to Great Britain. But in 1763, Parliament began increasing taxes on the colonies. Taxes were placed on items such as sugar, stamps, and tea. The colonists were unhappy. They protested the fact that they had no say in decisions that affected them. One of the most famous protests was the Boston Tea Party. On December 16, 1773, colonists dumped a shipment of tea into the Boston Harbor.

The British continued to create new taxes despite the colonists' protests. In September 1774, delegates from 12 colonies gathered

> The Boston Tea Party was a response to increasing taxes.

in Philadelphia, Pennsylvania. This meeting was called the First Continental Congress. The delegates agreed that King George III and Parliament needed to understand why the colonists were unhappy. The group sent a list of grievances to King George.

King George responded by sending troops to the colonies. They arrived in early 1775 prepared to crush the rebellion. Instead, they found the colonists ready to fight back.

The first shots of the American Revolution were fired at the Battle of Lexington.

On April 19, 1775, the first battle of the American Revolution (1775–1783) was fought in Lexington, Massachusetts. Soon, colonists would declare their freedom in writing.

12
Span of years in which new taxes were introduced.

- The most famous protest was the Boston Tea Party.
- The First Continental Congress met in Philadelphia.
- Lexington, Massachusetts, was the site of the first American Revolution battle.

GO TO THE SOURCE

To read the full text of the Declaration of Independence, go to **www.12StoryLibrary.com/primary**.

Why Did the Colonists Seek Independence?

The colonies were part of Great Britain. But some colonists felt cheated. People who lived in Great Britain had a voice in government matters. They were represented in Parliament. They could vote on taxes and other issues. The colonists did not get to vote for members of Parliament, so they were not represented. They believed they deserved the same rights. Without these rights, the colonists believed Parliament should not take their money. A common chant during this time was "No taxation without representation." The British did not agree, and the colonists began to yearn for independence.

Colonists had grown tired of following the laws of King George.

These feelings of independence were common in the eighteenth century. This era became known as

THINK ABOUT IT

It could take the British months traveling by boat on the Atlantic Ocean to get to the colonies. If you were a colonist, would you want to follow rules from a country far away? How would you go about making changes?

People took to the streets to protest unfair taxes.

the Age of Enlightenment. More people, especially those who lived in colonies, became concerned about individual rights. They did not want to follow the orders of a ruling country any longer. For many years, Parliament and King George had not bothered the colonies. The new taxes made individual rights and freedom an even more important cause for the colonists.

2
Number of months it could take for the British to travel across the Atlantic Ocean.

- The colonists were not represented in Parliament.
- A common chant in the 1700s was "No taxation without representation."
- The 1700s was known as the Age of Enlightenment.

What Is the Declaration of Independence?

The Declaration of Independence has been described in many ways throughout history. Most importantly, it is a legal document announcing that the 13 colonies were separating from Great Britain. It has also been called the birth certificate of the United States, marking the date when the nation was born. The Declaration of Independence was the founding document of the United States. It clearly states all the ideas the country was built on.

The Declaration of Independence was the colonists' way of explaining their decision to split from the British. The document included a list of grievances against Parliament and King George.

A common feeling at the time was that the colonies had to come together as one country if they were to survive.

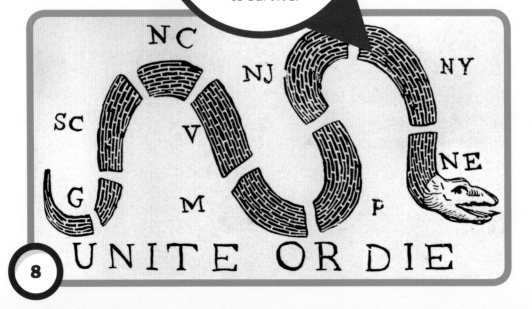

The colonists no longer wanted British troops—also called "redcoats"—on American soil.

These grievances detailed all the problems the colonists had with Great Britain. They wanted King George to know how upset they were.

The colonists no longer wanted political connections to Great Britain. This meant the removal of British troops from American soil. It also meant the loss of a trading partner. But for the first time it also meant the colonists could make decisions for their new nation. They could decide their individual rights and freedoms.

KING GEORGE III

George III became king in 1760, following the rule of his grandfather, George II. King George III's support of Parliament's taxation of the colonies led to the American Revolution. King George was unhappy when he read the Declaration of Independence. He did not like the colonies challenging his authority.

86
Number of changes made to the document before it was sent to King George.

- The Declaration of Independence is America's birth certificate.
- The document has all the ideas the country was founded on.
- The grievances listed in the document were against Parliament and King George.

4

Why Was the Declaration of Independence Written?

The 13 colonies had tried asking Parliament and King George to make changes. The First Continental Congress sent a list of their complaints. However, after no changes were made, tensions were rising. The colonists knew it was time for a big change.

The delegates met again in May 1775 at the Second Continental Congress in Philadelphia. In one last attempt to fix things, the delegates drafted the Olive Branch Petition. This document was sent to King George on July 8. It explained again why the colonists were upset. The delegates hoped it would show their loyalty to

The Declaration of Independence said the colonists wanted to break free from the British monarchy and govern themselves.

The colonists used the document to let the world know what their new country would stand for.

2.5 million

Estimated population of the colonies when the document was written.

- The Second Continental Congress met in May 1775.
- The delegates drafted the Olive Branch Petition, but King George refused to read it.
- The Declaration of Independence had groundbreaking ideas.

King George while also fixing issues. But King George refused to even read the petition.

That showed the colonists that King George would continue to ignore their individual rights. They needed to send a message to Parliament, the king, and other countries. The Declaration of Independence would be that message. The delegates wanted the new country's founding rights to include human equality. The delegates also wanted to move away from a monarchy. They thought people should choose who governed them. At the time this idea was groundbreaking. With these ideas and more in mind, the delegates needed someone to draft this important document.

5

Who Wrote the Declaration of Independence?

In June 1776, the Continental Congress met again. Richard Henry Lee, a delegate from Virginia, pushed for the Congress to declare independence from Great Britain. The Congress was already taking steps to do this. It created the Committee of Five to draft a statement that would later be called the Declaration of Independence. The committee included Thomas Jefferson, John Adams, Benjamin Franklin, Roger Sherman, and Robert Livingston.

The Congress took a break for three weeks to let the Committee of

From left, Franklin, Jefferson, Adams, Livingston, and Sherman formed the Committee of Five.

Five draft the document. Jefferson wrote most of it. He was chosen because of his background in political philosophy. After Jefferson finished his draft, Adams and Franklin made changes to key words and phrases. They also added to the list of charges against King George.

The Congress met on July 1, 1776. Over the next three days, members of the Continental Congress made more changes to the text. Finally,

Jefferson was credited with writing most of the Declaration of Independence.

the majority of the delegates approved the text. The Congress adopted the Declaration of Independence on July 4. The Committee of Five then took the manuscript to be printed and distributed. Copies of the Declaration of Independence were given to committees and commanders in the army.

Who Signed the Document?

The Continental Congress decided the Declaration of Independence should be handwritten for a final time on parchment. The title of the document was to be "The unanimous declaration of the thirteen United States of America." The Congress requested that all

Most of delegates gathered to sign the Declaration of Independence on August 2, 1776.

TIMING OF THE SIGNATURES

Not all members of the Congress signed the document on August 2. One signature was added on August 27, followed by three more on September 4. Another delegate signed on November 19. The final signature, from Thomas McKean, was not added until 1781. Some sources say it took him five years to sign because he was so busy.

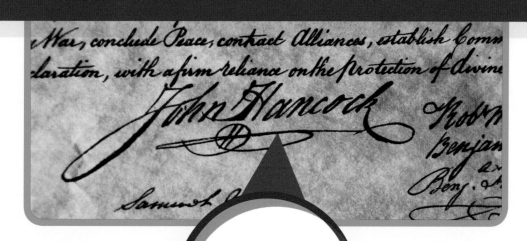

its members sign this copy.

Fifty-six men signed the Declaration of Independence. Each colony was represented by at least one signer. Most signed the document on August 2

Hancock's signature stands out from the rest.

at Independence Hall in Philadelphia. The signers of the Declaration of Independence came from different backgrounds. Many were from the upper class, while others were not. Some of the men had large families. Others were not married. The youngest signer, Edward Rutledge, was 26 years old. Benjamin Franklin was the oldest signer at 70. The largest signature on the document belongs to John Hancock. He served as president of the Continental Congress. Two of the signers would later become president of the United States—John Adams and Thomas Jefferson, both men who also helped draft this important document.

200
Approximate number of copies of the Declaration distributed before it was signed.

- The final handwritten document was written on July 19, 1776.
- The majority of the delegates signed on August 2.
- The youngest signer of the Declaration of Independence was 26 years old.

What Does the Declaration of Independence Say?

The Declaration of Independence is divided into five parts. These parts include the introduction, the preamble, the two sections of the body, and the conclusion. The introduction explains the reason for the document. It lists the problems that forced the colonies to seek independence. The introduction makes it clear that the British cannot do anything to change the colonists' minds. Next, the preamble lists the rights the United States is founded upon. Many of these are individual rights that focus on equality for all colonists. One of the most famous lines states that all Americans are "endowed by their Creator with certain unalienable Rights, that among these are Life, Liberty and the pursuit of Happiness."

The first section of the body is the longest part. It is a list of grievances against King George and Parliament.

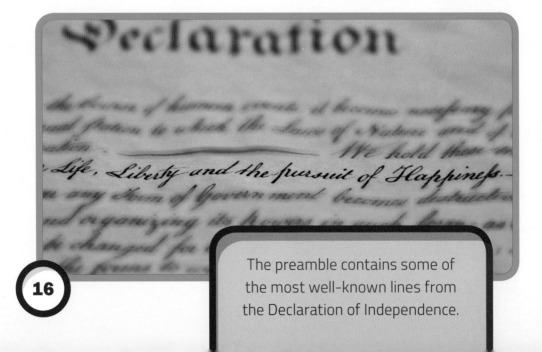

The preamble contains some of the most well-known lines from the Declaration of Independence.

TAKE NOTICE,

The colonists were prepared to fight if necessary to gain their freedom from King George.

These grievances are examples of how colonists felt their rights were violated. The colonists firmly believed King George and Parliament were suppressing their individual rights. The second section of the body lays out how the colonists tried to get the British to make changes.

The conclusion restates that King George is not fit to rule over the colonies. It also declares the colonies are free states without political connection to Great Britain.

THINK ABOUT IT

Follow the directions on page 5 to find the text from the Declaration of Independence. Read it carefully. Are there any other grievances you would add to the list? Do you think the document was clear about why the colonists were frustrated with Parliament and King George?

27
Number of grievances listed in the Declaration of Independence.

- The Declaration of Independence is divided into five parts.
- The preamble states the founding rights of the United States.
- The conclusion declares the colonies are free states.

Who Was the Declaration of Independence Written For?

In 1776, many colonists clearly were not happy with Great Britain. Numerous requests for change were ignored. The colonists knew they needed something bigger to get the attention of King George and Parliament. A legal document declaring the colonies were breaking away from Great Britain would surely do this.

Jefferson wrote a list of grievances in the Declaration of Independence. The other members of the Congress added to the list. These grievances were directed at King George. Many of the colonists were more upset with Parliament and its unfair taxation. But they did not direct their

Much of the colonists' anger came from unfair taxation such as the 1765 Stamp Act, which led to this protest in New York City.

THE FOLLY OF ENGLAND
AND THE RUIN OF AMERICA

Benjamin Franklin is shown returning from France, where he served nine years as an ambassador.

grievances at Parliament because they knew King George had the power to address their concerns.

The Declaration of Independence was mainly written for Parliament and King George. But it was also an announcement to the rest of the world. The colonists knew they would need support from other countries. Breaking ties with Great Britain meant losing military and financial support. The colonists hoped the Declaration of Independence would grab the attention of Great Britain's enemies. The new nation would need alliances and trading partners. Relationships with other countries suddenly became more vital to the survival of the United States.

26

Number of copies of the document made on July 4, 1776, that are known to sill exist.

- The Declaration of Independence was a legal document.
- The list of grievances was directed at King George even though colonists were more upset with Parliament.
- The Declaration of Independence was also an announcement to the world that the colonies were free states.

Where Did the Document Ideas Come From?

Thomas Jefferson did not come up with the ideas behind the Declaration of Independence on his own. Many of the concepts came from political philosophers and theorists from that era. Jefferson wanted the document to reflect the thoughts of all Americans, not just his own. Some of the philosophers Jefferson relied on for ideas included John Locke and Algernon Sidney. Jefferson also used notes from the Continental Congress meetings to draft

The writings of English philosophers such as Locke influenced Jefferson as he drafted the Declaration of Independence.

THINK ABOUT IT

Thomas Jefferson was tasked with writing one of the most important documents in US history. If you had to write an important document, would you use ideas from well-known people from history? Or would you create your own new ideas?

33

Jefferson's age when he wrote the Declaration of Independence.

- Many ideas in the document came from philosophers.
- Locke and Sidney were two of these philosophers.
- Jefferson used wording that was sometimes similar to the Virginia Declaration of Rights.

the Declaration of Independence.

Jefferson thought a lot about the language he would use. He knew this document would be read aloud many times in front of large crowds. He wanted the wording to be perfect. Jefferson thought about the sounds of the words and their rhythm as he wrote. To help with the wording of the Declaration of Independence, Jefferson looked at the Virginia

Mason wrote the Virginia Declaration of Rights, which also guided Jefferson's writing.

Declaration of Rights. George Mason wrote this document earlier in 1776. Some of the same phrases are used in both documents. Relying partly on thoughts and words from other sources, the Declaration of Independence had a large impact on the future.

10

What Was the Declaration of Independence's Impact?

The Declaration of Independence created a new nation. But it also had other lasting impacts around the world. The document was a symbol of equality. When the colonists determined they were not being treated as equals, they made changes to secure individual rights in the United States.

The Declaration of Independence would later be used in antislavery protests in 1829 by activist David Walker.

Leaders of the French Revolution were inspired by the American Revolution and the document that helped spark it.

DECLARATION OF SENTIMENTS

Many documents have been modeled after the Declaration of Independence. One is the Declaration of Sentiments, written in July 1848. Written by Elizabeth Cady Stanton, this important document states the rights women should have as US citizens. Stanton wrote about the struggles of women during the women's movement. At that time, women could not vote. They also had limited employment and educational opportunities.

Its echoes were heard in the fight for women's rights in 1848. Abraham Lincoln is thought to have read the Declaration of Independence before writing his famous Gettysburg Address. Martin Luther King Jr. cited the document in his famous "I Have a Dream" speech of 1963.

Outside of the United States, the Declaration of Independence also had an impact. Its ideas inspired other groups of people to fight for their independence. In France, Victor Riqueti quoted the Declaration of Independence during the French Revolution. Early in the nineteenth century, Colombians attempted to overthrow the Spanish empire in South America after hearing about the former colonies' new freedom.

Today, more than half of the 193 countries in the United Nations have some sort of founding document similar to the Declaration of Independence.

12

Number of colonies that immediately adopted the document on July 4, 1776.

- The Declaration of Independence was a symbol of equality.
- The document text was used in antislavery protests in 1829.
- The Declaration of Independence inspired people in other countries to seek independence from outside rulers.

Where Is the Original Document Kept?

The original Declaration of Independence is written on parchment. It is currently housed at the National Archives Building in Washington, DC. It has been there in a special protective case since 1952. But before the document arrived there, it traveled through several states and through several hands.

Most delegates signed the Declaration of Independence on August 2, 1776. Then, the document was filed in Philadelphia. It moved throughout the colonies when the Continental Congress moved. It landed back in Philadelphia and stayed there until 1800. Once the US Capitol was built, the Declaration of Independence document moved to Washington, DC. Under any threat of attack, the document was moved to safety. It was secured at Fort Knox, Kentucky, between 1941 and 1944 during World War II.

The National Archives Building in Washington, DC

The original Declaration of Independence is moved into place in the National Archives on December 13, 1952.

29.8
Length, in inches (75 cm), of the original Declaration of Independence.

The Declaration of Independence's final move was to the National Archives from the Library of Congress in 1952. The National Archives is the official building for all government records. It is also the most bombproof building in Washington, DC. This ensures this important document will always be safe.

- The original Declaration of Independence moved through many cities before settling in Washington, DC, in 1952.
- The document was moved to Fort Knox, Kentucky, during World War II.
- It is now housed with many other official government records and documents in the National Archives Building in Washington, DC.

What Does the
Document Mean Today?

The Declaration of Independence had a lasting impact on the date when the United States celebrates its birthday. Most of the delegates of the Continental Congress signed the document on August 2, 1776. But it was printed with the date "July 4" on it. This was the date the Congress adopted the document. Thus, Independence Day is celebrated every July 4. John Adams thought future Americans should celebrate Independence Day with parades, shows, bonfires, and fireworks. Americans do all of these things and more each summer.

Americans celebrate their independence on July 4, even though most of the delegates signed the Declaration of Independence on August 2.

But the Declaration of Independence represents more than just a holiday. It remains the very essence of what it means to be an American. The concepts of life, liberty, and happiness are frequently mentioned in modern political arguments. They are often cited by minority groups

The Declaration of Independence reminds us of the sacrifices the colonists made to secure their freedoms.

seeking equal treatment under the law. The Declaration of Independence stands as a reminder of the freedoms the colonists fought for. And it helps remind Americans today that they should not take those freedoms for granted.

1938

Year July 4 became a paid holiday for employees of the federal government.

- Adams thought future Americans should celebrate Independence Day.
- The first July 4 celebrations were in 1777 in Philadelphia.
- The Declaration of Independence reminds Americans of the freedoms the colonists fought for.

Fact Sheet

- Independence Hall was home to the signing of the Declaration of Independence and the US Constitution, both founding documents of the United States. The building was originally built for Pennsylvania's colonial government. Today, people can visit this historic building in Philadelphia.

- Many of the men who signed the Declaration of Independence also signed other historic documents. Some of these documents included the Articles of Confederation, the US Constitution, and the Articles of Association.

- In 1989, a man at a flea market bought a frame that contained one of the original Declaration of Independence copies in the back. This copy was sold in 2000 for $8.14 million.

- The original Declaration of Independence is housed in a special case in Washington, DC. The case has a titanium frame with laminated, antireflective glass. It also blocks ultraviolet rays. Bombs, bullets, and even hurricanes cannot break the case surrounding the document.

- The original 26 copies of the Declaration of Independence that exist are called the Dunlap Broadside. John Dunlap printed these copies on July 4. American institutions own 21 copies. British organizations own two other copies, while the final three copies have private owners. Many replicas have been made over the years for souvenirs or for display purposes.

Glossary

Age of Enlightenment
An era during the eighteenth and nineteenth centuries when cultural and intellectual forces influenced reason, analysis, and individual rights.

colony
A country or area under the full or partial political control of another country, typically a distant one, and occupied by settlers from that country.

delegates
Representatives chosen to act for others at a convention.

grievances
Statements that explain why a person or people are not satisfied with something.

independence
When a country gains political freedom from other control.

monarchy
A form of government in which a country is ruled by a king or queen.

parchment
Paper made from sheepskin or goatskin.

Parliament
The government of Great Britain.

philosophy
Ideas about knowledge, truth, and other parts of life.

preamble
A statement made at the beginning of a document that usually gives the reason for the text that follows.

rebelling
Opposing a government or ruler.

unalienable
Impossible to take away.

For More Information

Books

Betti, Matthew. *The Declaration of Independence and the Continental Congress.* New York: PowerKids, 2016.

Gagne, Tammy. *The Story of the Declaration of Independence.* Hockessin, DE: Mitchell Lane, 2016.

Marcovitz, Hal. *The Declaration of Independence: Forming a New Nation.* Philadelphia, PA: Mason Crest, 2015.

Wolfe, James, and Jennifer Viegas. *Understanding the Declaration of Independence.* New York: Enslow, 2016.

Visit 12StoryLibrary.com

Scan the code or use your school's login at **12StoryLibrary.com** for recent updates about this topic and a full digital version of this book. Enjoy free access to:

- Digital ebook
- Breaking news updates
- Live content feeds
- Videos, interactive maps, and graphics
- Additional web resources

Note to educators: Visit 12StoryLibrary.com/register to sign up for free premium website access. Enjoy live content plus a full digital version of every 12-Story Library book you own for every student at your school.

Index

About the Author

Mirella S. Miller is an author and editor of several children's books. She lives in Minnesota with her husband and their dog.

READ MORE FROM 12-STORY LIBRARY

Every 12-Story Library book is available in many formats. For more information, visit 12StoryLibrary.com.